The Happy Ones

by Julie Marie Myatt

A SAMUEL FRENCH ACTING EDITION

SAMUEL FRENCH

FOUNDED 1830

NEW YORK HOLLYWOOD LONDON TORONTO

SAMUELFRENCH.COM

Copyright © 2010 by Julie Marie Myatt

ALL RIGHTS RESERVED

Cover image provided by
South Coast Repertory / Benjamin Horak

CAUTION: Professionals and amateurs are hereby warned that *THE HAPPY ONES* is subject to a Licensing Fee. It is fully protected under the copyright laws of the United States of America, the British Commonwealth, including Canada, and all other countries of the Copyright Union. All rights, including professional, amateur, motion picture, recitation, lecturing, public reading, radio broadcasting, television and the rights of translation into foreign languages are strictly reserved. In its present form the play is dedicated to the reading public only.

The amateur and professional live stage performance rights to *THE HAPPY ONES* are controlled exclusively by Samuel French, Inc., and licensing arrangements and performance licenses must be secured well in advance of presentation. PLEASE NOTE that amateur Licensing Fees are set upon application in accordance with your producing circumstances. When applying for a licensing quotation and a performance license please give us the number of performances intended, dates of production, your seating capacity and admission fee. Licensing Fees are payable one week before the opening performance of the play to Samuel French, Inc., at 45 W. 25th Street, New York, NY 10010.

Licensing Fee of the required amount must be paid whether the play is presented for charity or gain and whether or not admission is charged.

Stock/professional licensing fees quoted upon application to Samuel French, Inc.

For all other rights than those stipulated above, apply to: Bret Adams, Ltd, 448 West 44th Street, New York, NY 10036, Attn: Bruce Ostler.

Particular emphasis is laid on the question of amateur or professional readings, permission and terms for which must be secured in writing from Samuel French, Inc.

Copying from this book in whole or in part is strictly forbidden by law, and the right of performance is not transferable.

Whenever the play is produced the following notice must appear on all programs, printing and advertising for the play: "Produced by special arrangement with Samuel French, Inc."

Due authorship credit must be given on all programs, printing and advertising for the play.

ISBN 978-0-573-69871-2   Printed in U.S.A.   #29676

No one shall commit or authorize any act or omission by which the copyright of, or the right to copyright, this play may be impaired.

No one shall make any changes in this play for the purpose of production.

Publication of this play does not imply availability for performance. Both amateurs and professionals considering a production are strongly advised in their own interests to apply to Samuel French, Inc., for written permission before starting rehearsals, advertising, or booking a theatre.

No part of this book may be reproduced, stored in a retrieval system, or transmitted in any form, by any means, now known or yet to be invented, including mechanical, electronic, photocopying, recording, videotaping, or otherwise, without the prior written permission of the publisher.

MUSIC USE NOTE

Licensees are solely responsible for obtaining formal written permission from copyright owners to use copyrighted music in the performance of this play and are strongly cautioned to do so. If no such permission is obtained by the licensee, then the licensee must use only original music that the licensee owns and controls. Licensees are solely responsible and liable for all music clearances and shall indemnify the copyright owners of the play and their licensing agent, Samuel French, Inc., against any costs, expenses, losses and liabilities arising from the use of music by licensees.

IMPORTANT BILLING AND CREDIT REQUIREMENTS

All producers of *THE HAPPY ONES* *must* give credit to the Author of the Play in all programs distributed in connection with performances of the Play, and in all instances in which the title of the Play appears for the purposes of advertising, publicizing or otherwise exploiting the Play and/or a production. The name of the Author *must* appear on a separate line on which no other name appears, immediately following the title and *must* appear in size of type not less than fifty percent of the size of the title type.

In addition the following credit *must* be given in all programs and publicity information distributed in association with this piece on the title page of the program and on the presentation page of the publication:

The Happy Ones was commissioned and first produced
By South Coast Repertory

THE HAPPY ONES was first produced by the South Coast Repertory in Costa Mesa, California on September 27, 2009. The performance was directed by Martin Benson, with scenic design by Ralph Funicello, costume design by Angela Balogh Calin, lighting design by Tom Ruzika, sound design by Paul James Prendergast, and dramaturgy by John Glore. The production stage manager was Jennifer Ellen Butler, and the associate director was Oahn Nguyen. The cast was as follows:

MARY ELLEN HUGHES	Nike Doukas
GARY STUART	Geoffrey Lower
WALTER WELLS	Raphael Sbarge
BAO NGO	Greg Watanabe

THE HAPPY ONES was the winner of the 2009 Ted Schmitt Award for the world premiere of an Outstanding New Play – Los Angeles Drama Critics Circle.

CHARACTERS

Walter Wells
Bao Ngo
Minister Gary Stuart
Mary-Ellen Hughes

SETTING

Orange County, California

TIME

1975, 1976

"We hold these truths to be self-evident, that all men are created equal, that they are endowed by their Creator with certain unalienable Rights, that among these are Life, Liberty and the pursuit of Happiness."

U.S. Declaration of Independence

ACT 1

Scene One

(Lights up on:)

(The living room of the beautiful new suburban/planned community home of **WALTER WELLS**. *It's August, 1975.)*

(A large family portrait hangs over the couch. A Sears-style posed photograph.)

(The sound of kids playing outside.)

(WALTER WELLS *sets up the house for a party. He organizes his liquor bottles. Admires his bar. He shouts toward the kitchen.)*

WALTER. How's it going in there? Honey?

(He listens.)

Margaret? You ready?

MARGARET. *(offstage)* Put on some music, will you please?

WALTER. What?

MARGARET. *(offstage)* Music please?

WALTER. You need help?

MARGARET. *(offstage)* I need some music and a cocktail, please!

WALTER. You need help? People are coming any minute –

MARGARET. *(offstage)* Cocktail, honey! And please get the kids out of the pool!

*(***WALTER** *opens a sliding glass door.)*

WALTER. Hey kids! Get out of the pool! Time to get dressed! People are coming soon!

KIDS. *(offstage)* No!

WALTER. Yes. It's your mother's birthday. C'mon now.

KIDS. *(offstage)* No!

WALTER. OK. Three more minutes. Then I want you to come in and get dressed in your good clothes. And please don't get water everywhere coming in here.

(He watches the kids. Claps his hands.)

WALTER. Nice swimming there, Danny! Looking good, son! Don't, don't…don't forget to breathe. Hey, Lisa! Lisa! Make sure your brother breathes, will you, sweetheart? And be careful. No, no running.

LISA. *(offstage)* Did you see my dive, Dad?

WALTER. I sure did. That was wonderful. That's what you call a swan dive. Fantastic.

LISA. *(offstage)* I'm gonna do it again.

WALTER. OK. But careful. No crazy stuff. I don't want you to get hurt.

*(**WALTER** closes the door and puts a record on his new stereo. Admires his stereo, cleans off a speck of dust. A rock song, something like "Spirit in the Sky" by Norman Greenbaum plays loud.)**

*(**WALTER** moves with the music.)*

(He tries one of the appetizers on the table. And then another.)

(He makes martinis. Shakes it to the music. Tastes it. Delicious.)

(Pours two glasses.)

(Little dance.)

(He checks on the kids again. Opens door.)

Two more minutes! Swim like you mean it!

(He closes the door.)

(Straighten a picture.)

(Little dance. Grabs cocktail to bring to Margaret.)

(The doorbell rings.)

Honey?

---

* Please see Music Use Note on page 3.

MARGARET. *(offstage)* I'm not ready!

WALTER. They're here.

MARGARET. *(offstage)* Get that please!

WALTER. You want me to bring me your –

MARGARET. *(offstage)* Get the door, Walter!

WALTER. Happy Birthday!

MARGARET. *(offstage)* I'm not ready!

WALTER. I love you!

(The doorbell rings again.)

(He exits to get the door.)

(Music plays softly under the next scene.)

Scene Two

(Outside a church.)

*(**WALTER** stands with the **MINISTER GARY STUART**, waiting for, and waving to, the congregation as they arrive. **GARY** wears sunglasses.)*

GARY. Great party last night.

WALTER. Wasn't it fantastic?

GARY. Man. Whew.

WALTER. I think that was our best one yet.

GARY. Definitely. Whew. You survive alright?

WALTER. I never felt better. You?

GARY. The sermon could be on the brief side this morning.

WALTER. What's the topic?

GARY. Moderation.

*(**GARY** adjusts his sunglasses.)*

Where's Margaret?

WALTER. Still in bed. We finished the gin.

GARY. Ah.

WALTER. Danced until five. Then watched the sun come up from the roof. Who was that in the pool with you last night?

GARY. Mary-Ellen Hughes.

WALTER. Who's that?

GARY. Divorced. Just moved to the neighborhood. That green house.

WALTER. She likes to have a good time.

GARY. Yes, she does.

(silence)

Yes, she does.

WALTER. Didn't Margaret look gorgeous last night?

GARY. Extremely.

WALTER. She is getting more beautiful by the day and I'm getting more middle-aged.

GARY. Yep.

WALTER. The kids are lucky they take after her.

GARY. They are.

WALTER. Sweet, good-looking.

GARY. Polite.

WALTER. You think so?

GARY. Oh yeah. Absolutely.

WALTER. I appreciate that. Really, you think so?

GARY. Absolutely.

(**GARY** *waves to someone offstage.*)

WALTER. I think they're polite and well-mannered, but you know, no one's ever really honest with you about your kids. They'll lie to your face.

GARY. How many martinis did I have last night?

WALTER. I couldn't tell you.

GARY. You were the bartender.

WALTER. I lost count.

(**GARY** *pulls back his collar.*)

GARY. Do I have a hicky on my neck?

WALTER. What was her name again?

GARY. Mary-Ellen.

WALTER. I think I found her top in the pool this morning.

GARY. Really?

WALTER. Where'd you meet her?

(**GARY** *waves to another person offstage.*)

GARY. I married her and her ex years ago.

(**WALTER** *waves to the same person.*)

He was an hour late. He refused to repeat after me. Then he dropped the ring on the floor, and asked her to pick it up.

WALTER. Did she?

GARY. Nope. Nope. Longest ceremony of my life.

(*They both wave to a few people offstage.*)

GARY. *(cont.)* But now. She's here in town. Free as a bird.

(silence)

Free as a bird.

(GARY *waves to one more person.)*

(WALTER *takes it all in; this beautiful day, his great life.)*

WALTER. You know….we have got it made, Gary.

GARY. Yes we do.

WALTER. Beautiful women. Beautiful children. Great neighbors. Fantastic jobs. Gorgeous weather.

(GARY *feels a wave of nausea; still suffering his hangover.)*

GARY. Praise God.

WALTER. Praise California.

(silence)

WALTER. This is living.

GARY. Yes, it is.

WALTER. Seriously. This is the dream right here. We got it.

(WALTER *puts on his sunglasses.)*

This is it.

Scene Three

(Wells Appliance Store)

(**WALTER** *takes inventory.*)

(Phone rings.)

WALTER. Wells Appliance. Oh, hello, John. How are you? How are the kids? Uh huh…Uh huh…Fantastic. Wonderful. Yes. How many you need?…Uh huh… We've got it. Yep, got that too. I'll have it sent over this afternoon. You're off Euclid, right? Brookhurst. Darn it. That's right. I knew that. Brookhurst…OK then. Sure will. Say hello to Helen. Uh huh. Bye. Bye.

(He hangs up.)

(The phone rings again.)

Wells Appliance. This is Walter. Well, how are you, Sandra? It was a fantastic party. Thank you. Yeah. Uh huh. I know…We all tied one on…Uh huh…Uh huh…Yeah…That dishwasher's working out for you then? Wonderful. Marvelous. Oh you do? Great. Well, we have the fridge in Avocado. Yeah. Want me to put that on lay-away for you? Sure. Sure. I can do that. No problem. Fantastic. OK. OK then. Tell Richard I'll see him on the golf course on Saturday. Uh huh. Uh huh. Wonderful. OK. Uh huh. You too. Bye Bye.

(He writes down the order.)

(The phone rings again.)

Wells Appliance…Yes. I have Prince Albert in a can. But I'm sorry, he can't be reached at the moment.

(He hangs up.)

(The phone rings again.)

Wells Appliance…Listen, actually, he's *on* the can, and he's asked you to please not bother him again. He doesn't like to talk about it, but I'll be frank with you, kid. He's extremely constipated. And interruptions such as these ruin his concentration.

(He hangs up.)

(The phone rings again.)

WALTER. *(cont.) (British accent)* Prince Albert here…This is extremely poor timing –
(his own voice) This is Wells Appliance. This is Walter Wells…No really, seriously, this is him, I'm Walter Wells…Yes…Yes…What?

(silence)

Are, are you sure it was my family…

(He sits down, listening.)

Where?…

(long silence)

I'm, I'm still here.

Scene Four

*(**GARY** enters in a black suit and help dress **WALTER** for the funeral. **GARY** ties **WALTER**'s tie, adjust **WALTER**'s shirt collar, and helps **WALTER** put on his own black suit jacket.)*

Scene Five

(Wells living room)

(**WALTER** *enters in his black suit.)*

(That large family portrait smiles into the room.)

(He looks around at his perfect, empty house.)

(His daughter's Barbie doll left on a shelf.)

(His son's fake sword on the floor. Next to a tiny car.)

(His wife's shoes beside the couch.)

(He sits down on his couch, unsure of what to do next. Lost.)

(He finds one of his son's toys in the cushion of the couch.)

Scene Six

(Hospital)

*(**BAO NGO** lays in bed connected to machines and IVs. One arm is broken. His face is bruised. Bandage on his chest.)*

*(**WALTER** enters.)*

*(He meets eyes with **BAO**.)*

(silence)

*(More silence, as **WALTER** tries to figure out what to say next.)*

*(**WALTER** slowly approaches him.)*

WALTER. The signs told you it was the wrong way.

(silence)

It was the wrong way. Can't you read?

(silence)

They weren't doing anything to hurt you. They were just trying to get home.

(silence)

That's all.

(silence)

Couldn't you have stayed home? Huh? Is that too much to ask? Stay home. Stay away from the car. Stay away from the freeway. Stay away from my wife. Stay away from my kids. Stay away from my life. If you had never come, I would have my family…so go…Go back to Vietnam…No one wants you here.

*(**BAO** begins to pull out all the needles and wires.)*

Hey. Hey.

*(**WALTER** rushes over and tries to stop him.)*

What are you doing?

BAO. I want to die.

WALTER. Stop that.

BAO. I want to die.

WALTER. Stop.

BAO. No.

(*WALTER grabs BAO's hands.*)

WALTER. Nurse!

BAO. Kill me.

WALTER. Nurse!

BAO. Kill me. Please.

WALTER. No.

BAO. I don't want to live anymore.

WALTER. Too bad. Nurse!

BAO. Please.

(*The men stare at each other.*)

I have enough.

(*silence*)

I'm sorry.

(*WALTER lets him go.*)

(*BAO rips at his bandages. More wires.*)

(*WALTER grabs him again.*)

WALTER. Nurse!

BAO. Let me die.

WALTER. Nurse! Goddamnit!

BAO. Let me die now. I have had enough.

(*WALTER holds him down.*)

WALTER. Nurse!

BAO. I've had enough.

WALTER. Nurse!

(*WALTER continues to hold him on the bed.*)

BAO. Please. I've had enough.

WALTER. Nurse!

Scene Seven

(Wells living room.)

(Night.)

(WALTER *sits drinking with* **GARY** *on the couch.)*

(Long silence.)

(GARY *refills their glasses.)*

WALTER. I have done everything right in my life. Everything. Haven't I?

GARY. Yes.

WALTER. I am the luckiest man I know. I've won every raffle I ever entered. Could play every sport I ever tried. (Except lacrosse.)

*(**GARY** nods.)*

Elected class president in my high school *and* college. Got the girl of my dreams. Got a son *and* a daughter. Right?

GARY. Yes.

WALTER. Built my own business. Nothing bad has ever happened to me. I have been a good citizen. A good husband. A good father. A good business man. A good Christian. A good neighbor. Haven't I?

GARY. Yes.

(silence)

WALTER. Was it not enough?

GARY. Of course, that's not the –

WALTER. Was I too happy?

GARY. No.

WALTER. Is it just my turn?

GARY. No.

WALTER. Was it little Danny's turn? Or Lisa's? Or Margaret? They were just sweet, innocent people. Harmless. How could they deserve that?

GARY. They don't – they didn't.

WALTER. What kind of God lets a man go the wrong way on
a fucking freeway exit, hit three innocent people head
on, and then *live*? Huh?

(silence)

GARY. The same God that lets bombs drop on his people, I
guess. I don't know.

WALTER. Don't give me that bullshit.

GARY. I don't understand why God does what he does –

WALTER. *I* didn't drop those bombs.

GARY. I know –

WALTER. My family didn't.

GARY. I know.

WALTER. Don't bring the war into this. I had nothing to do
with that. That man's people has nothing to do with
me.

GARY. I know, I just –

WALTER. Is this how they teach you to counsel the grieving in seminary? Seriously, they give you a manual or
something –

GARY. I'm sorry, I'm terrible at this, I know, but I'm just –

WALTER. *Unitarians.* Typical.

GARY. All I'm trying to say…what am I trying to say?…

(silence)

Hating that man will do you no good, Walter.

WALTER. What page is that on in the manual? 44?

GARY. It was an accident.

WALTER. I know –

GARY. He is suffering, too.

WALTER. You don't know what this feels like –

GARY. You're right. I don't. I can only imagine that it is
more painful than I could ever imagine.

WALTER. It's worse.

*(**GARY** finishes his drink.)*

GARY. I think God is a real asshole sometimes. I really do. Which makes me useless at this part of my job. But, hating the man that killed your family, won't get you anything. Nothing worth keeping. You're a better person than that.

WALTER. How do you know?

(The doorbell rings.)

(Neither man makes a move.)

(It rings again.)

WALTER. Please get that.

(GARY *goes to answer the door.)*

WALTER. Tell them I'm not taking visitors.

(WALTER *looks around his house.)*

(GARY *returns with a casserole.)*

WALTER. You've got lipstick on your lips.

GARY. It was Mary-Ellen.

(He wipes his lips.)

WALTER. What is it?

GARY. Tuna something.

WALTER. Gezz.

GARY. What?

WALTER. There are four of those in the fridge already.

GARY. It's the thought –

WALTER. In what world does a man whose just lost his entire life want to eat canned tuna with noodles and mushroom soup? Tell me?

GARY. I will tell her you loved it.

WALTER. Why don't you take it.

GARY. No.

WALTER. Take it.

GARY. I don't want it.

WALTER. Please.

GARY. She made it for you.

WALTER. Take it.

GARY. She made it for you.

WALTER. Just take it.

GARY. I don't want to.

WALTER. She's a terrible cook, isn't she?

(silence)

GARY. She is very creative…in her cuisine.

WALTER. Margaret is a fantastic cook.

(silence)

She was wonderful, wasn't she, Gary?

GARY. One of the best women I've ever met.

WALTER. And my kids? They were perfect, weren't they?

GARY. Absolutely.

WALTER. I had everything I wanted. Everything.

(silence)

And he killed it.

Scene Eight

(Wells living room)

(Morning)

(The door bell rings.)

(WALTER *is crashed out in his clothes on the couch.)*

WALTER. What?

(The door bell rings again.)

What? Dammit. What?

(MARY-ELLEN *enters with a bag of potato chips.)*

MARY-ELLEN. The door was open so...I let myself in. Obviously.

(She smiles.)

Mary-Ellen. Hughes.

(She reaches out to shake his hand.)

I was at your party, but we didn't get a chance to meet.

WALTER. I remember.

MARY-ELLEN. What did I do?

WALTER. Uh –

MARY-ELLEN. Did I make a fool of myself?

WALTER. No –

MARY-ELLEN. Is that why you remember me? Did I do something embarrassing?

WALTER. No –

MARY-ELLEN. I asked Gary what I did because actually I blacked out that night, and I didn't realize I had blacked out until I couldn't remember how I got home the next morning, and then Gary said he brought me home, so I thought, well, he's a minister so I guess he wouldn't lie, would he?

WALTER. No.

MARY-ELLEN. What'd I do?

WALTER. Nothing.

MARY-ELLEN. Did I kiss you?

WALTER. No.

MARY-ELLEN. Did I take my shirt off?

WALTER. No.

MARY-ELLEN. Are you sure? It's blue. I can't find it –

WALTER. Uh huh.

MARY-ELLEN. Did I sing?

WALTER. No –

MARY-ELLEN. Did I dance real sexy? I've been known to do that too.

WALTER. No.

MARY-ELLEN. Are you sure?

WALTER. Yes.

(She smiles, wipes her forehead.)

MARY-ELLEN. New girl doesn't want to look like a floozy. I mean, I'm divorced and that's bad enough, but you know, acting like a drunk stripper doesn't help me make friends with the women in the neighborhood.

WALTER. I guess not.

MARY-ELLEN. Doesn't hurt with the men though.

WALTER. No.

MARY-ELLEN. And that's not a come on. Honest. It's just a fact.

WALTER. It is.

MARY-ELLEN. I'm not proud of it. But, I like to have fun What can I say. Shoot me. You only live once.

(silence)

I like your house.

WALTER. Thank you.

MARY-ELLEN. I think you've got a nicer floor plan than I've got. Of course, it's just me, so I don't need all those bedrooms....

(MARY-ELLEN looks at the large family portrait. Making her way into the conversation....)

MARY-ELLEN. *(cont.)* I'm so sorry about what happened, Walter. Really. You must be...you just must be unbelievably sad.

(silence)

My baby brother was killed in Vietnam five years ago and I didn't get out of bed for two months. It was awful. And no one understands what you're going through. No one.

WALTER. No.

MARY-ELLEN. I lived on saltine crackers. That's all I could eat. And vodka. Lost fifteen pounds. I guess there was an up-side. And my marriage went to hell. Actually, that was an upside too. He was kind of a jerk. He had money, but did not like to have fun. So I learned. The hard way. But, divorce bought me a house. Another upside. That silver lining is blinding! Anyway...enough about me.

(She hands him the potato chips.)

I forgot to put these on your casserole. You're supposed to crunch them up and put them on top.

WALTER. Thanks.

MARY-ELLEN. I prefer to layer them in.

WALTER. I see.

MARY-ELLEN. I ate half the bag last night. Sorry.

WALTER. That's fine.

MARY-ELLEN. "Can't eat just one."

(She smiles.)

I should have brought you some coffee. You want me to make a pot?

WALTER. No, no. That's OK.

MARY-ELLEN. Please. It's the least I could do. Standing here, jabbering on about myself first thing in the morning. I'll make you a pot of coffee before I go.

WALTER. No –

MARY-ELLEN. Sit.

(She exits into the kitchen.)

(WALTER *sits back down on the couch with the chips.)*

(He keeps looking toward the kitchen, finally she emerges with a plate of banana bread.)

I love your kitchen. I'd kill for that new oven. OK. So. Coffee is on. And here's a little something to go with it. The name "Carol Martin" was taped to the side of the foil, which makes me assume she made it and wanted you to know she made it. She clutches her husband like a cheetah every time I walk by, and refuses to talk to me in complete sentences, or look me in the eye, but, it appears she can bake a decent banana bread.

WALTER. You really didn't need to –

MARY-ELLEN. Please please.

(She grabs his shoulders.)

Now listen to me, Mr. Walter Wells. Here's what I want you to do: Cry your guts out. Stay in bed. Don't shower. Don't bathe. Drink heavily. Smoke dope. Pop pills. Chew tobacco. Do whatever you need to do, but don't you dare be ashamed of how sad and lonely and angry you feel. Alright? It's no one's business how you do this.

WALTER. OK.

MARY-ELLEN. And call if you need anything. Really. Because I love to drink and smoke and cry, and I'm really good at all three. Together or separate. I'm a pro. But that's not a come on, Walter. Honest. I'm seeing Gary. You know that, right?

WALTER. I do.

MARY-ELLEN. Did he tell you that?

WALTER. Not in so many words, but yes.

MARY-ELLEN. What did he say?

WALTER. Well –

MARY-ELLEN. I really have no idea how that man became a minister. Honest. He's about as close to a saint as I am. And the only reason either of us gets on our knees is not for God, I'll tell you that much.

(Checks her watch.)

Shoot. I gotta get to work. My boss is a clock watcher. You take care of yourself. I mean it.

(She rushes out.)

(**WALTER** *lays back down on the couch.*)

("Long As I Can See the Light" by Creedance Clearwater Revival plays.)*

---

* Please see Music Use Note on page 3.

Scene Nine

(Wells Appliance)

(**WALTER** *looks over his bills.*)

(The phone rings.)

(He turns down the radio.)

WALTER. Wells Appliance…No.

(He hangs up.)

(Phone rings again. He answers it.)

You gotta get a new joke, kid. This "Prince Albert in a can" is a little long in the tooth, you know – Oh hello, Pete. Sorry about that. I got this regular crank caller…. I appreciate that…Well, I was home, but I couldn't stay away from work, you know how it is…Business can't run itself…uh huh…uh huh…Right…What can I do for you?…Uh huh…yeah…what size you looking for?

(**BAO** *enters.*)

Is, uh, is, is this going to be billed to the contractor or the housing development?…OK…Great…Listen, this is all fantastic. I just need to help a customer real quick, can I call you back?…OK, I'll call you back. Thanks, Pete.

(**WALTER** *hangs up the phone.*)

WALTER. What do you want?

BAO. I, I want to talk to you.

WALTER. Why?

BAO. I want –

WALTER. I don't want to talk to you.

BAO. This is a very nice store.

WALTER. And if you want to buy an appliance, you can go somewhere else.

BAO. No. I don't want your appliance. But they are very nice.

(silence)

BAO. *(cont.)* If wanted an appliance, I would buy it here.
(silence)
I would.

WALTER. You decided not to kill yourself?

(**BAO** *shows him his wrists. Bandages on each.*)

What happened?

(**BAO** *smiles.*)

BAO. I'm a coward.

(**WALTER** *just looks at him.*)

I want to help you.

WALTER. You want to help me? Do what?

BAO. I don't have money, but in Vietnam I have many skill.
I am a doctor.

WALTER. Not interested.

BAO. And I'm a good cook too.

WALTER. I don't need a doctor or a cook.

BAO. I can also make a garden. Grow food.

WALTER. I go to the store for that.

BAO. I know how to paint pictures.

WALTER. I have enough pictures.

BAO. I can clean house.

WALTER. I don't need a maid.

BAO. I can wash your car.

WALTER. You're not going near my car or house or life –

BAO. I can cut hair.

WALTER. Knock it off.

BAO. I can sew.

WALTER. Knock it off.

BAO. I am a good dancer –

WALTER. I said, knock it off.

(silence)

If you've come here looking for a job, you have a lot of
fucking nerve.

BAO. I don't want a job.

WALTER. I don't have anything to give you.

BAO. I don't want anything –

WALTER. I gave you my family, isn't that enough?

(silence)

BAO. I want to give you something.

WALTER. No.

BAO. Please. I will not ask you to forgive me. I will not ask. I know I'm going to hell. I am sorry for what I do to you. Let me give you something.

WALTER. No.

BAO. Please.

*(***BAO*** gets on his knees.)*

Please. I must give you something. If I have to live, let me give you something.

WALTER. Get up –

BAO. I'm alive, so I give you something to help you. I give you something. Food. Can I give you food?

WALTER. Get up.

BAO. I'll make you food, OK?

WALTER. Get up.

BAO. Please let me give you something, OK? I clean your house.

*(***WALTER*** pulls him off the floor.)*

*(***BAO*** hangs on ***WALTER***'s arm.)*

Please. I need to give you something. Before I go to hell.

WALTER. Just stop the hell talk. Please. I really don't like it –

(The phone rings.)

*(***WALTER*** answers.)*

Wells Appliance…Can I call you back, Gary?…I'm fine…I can't talk right now…I'll call you back.

(He hangs up.)

(**BAO** *lets go of* **WALTER**.)

(*The two men aren't sure what to do next.*)

BAO. Please. I want to die. I try. I can't die. OK. So I think. What can I do? I can help this man. I give him something. Anything. Please.

WALTER. Listen…

BAO. Please.

(*silence*)

WALTER. You can't, you can't repay me for killing my family. It doesn't work that way.

BAO. I'm not repay. Not that. I just want to give you something. Please –

WALTER. Let me put it more bluntly: I'm not interested in having any contact with you. At all.

BAO. OK.

WALTER. OK.

BAO. You don't need to see me. I help you, but you don't need to see me. That's good plan.

(**WALTER** *sighs loudly.*)

BAO. Good plan, OK?

WALTER. No. Not a good plan.

BAO. Yes. I come to your house when you're not there. You never see me. I'm invisible.

WALTER. How about you leave now, and I never see you again.

BAO. Not a good plan. No.

WALTER. I don't want to see you.

(*The telephone rings.*)

BAO. I am invisible. I promise.

WALTER. Wells Appliance…Gary –

BAO. Please.

WALTER. I told you I'd call you back. I'm fine…Stop bugging me.

BAO. I'm invisible.

(He hangs up.)

(The phone rings again.)

WALTER. I AM FINE, GARY!

(BAO *is back on his knees, begging.)*

BAO. Please.

(WALTER *hangs up the phone.)*

Please. I help you.

WALTER. Get up.

BAO. I'm invisible.

(The phone rings again.)

I have to help you.

WALTER. Get up. Please.

BAO. I have to help you.

(BAO *is holding on to* **WALTER,** *begging.)*

WALTER. Jesus Christ.

BAO. Please. I'm invisible. I promise.

(The phone rings again.)

Scene Ten

(Wells living room)

*(***WALTER*** *enters and sits in front of the TV with a plate of Vietnamese food.)*

(There are fresh flowers on the table.)

*(***GARY*** *enters with* ***MARY-ELLEN****.)*

MARY-ELLEN. Smells good in here.

WALTER. I didn't hear the doorbell.

GARY. Oh, we didn't ring it.

WALTER. Why not?

GARY. The door was unlocked.

MARY-ELLEN. What is that?

WALTER. I don't know what it's called. I really wish you'd ring the bell –

MARY-ELLEN. Is it Chinese?

WALTER. Uh. Yeah.

GARY. Where'd you get it?

WALTER. I bought it.

GARY. Looks good.

WALTER. I'd really like to be alone.

MARY-ELLEN. Can I try it?

*(***WALTER*** *pushes it towards her.)*

WALTER. Don't you two have other things to do?

GARY. No.

MARY-ELLEN. This is delicious. Oh Gary, try it.

WALTER. Seriously, I really want to be left alone.

GARY. Wow. I've never tasted anything like that.

MARY-ELLEN. That just says more, doesn't it?

WALTER. It's late. I want to go to bed.

GARY. Spicy.

WALTER. Please.

GARY. Wow.

WALTER. I want to go to bed.

MARY-ELLEN. Oh, Walter. We just went to hear Joan Baez at Melodyland. Oh my goodness, you should have gone. She was wonderful.

GARY. Mary-Ellen –

MARY-ELLEN. "The water is wide, I cannot get over, and neither have I wings to fly…"

GARY. Mary-Ellen –

MARY-ELLEN. "Give me a boat –

(WALTER exits.)

GARY. I told you Walter gave me the tickets.

MARY-ELLEN. No you didn't.

GARY. Yes. I did. Margaret had bought them for their anniversary.

(silence)

MARY-ELLEN. Well. I'm a jerk.

GARY. Yeah.

(silence)

MARY-ELLEN. I don't remember you telling me that.

GARY. I did. Let's go.

(MARY-ELLEN looks around room.)

MARY-ELLEN. Did Walter get a housekeeper?

GARY. Not that I know of.

MARY-ELLEN. Looks awfully clean in here.

GARY. Maybe he cleaned it.

MARY-ELLEN. Fresh flowers? He didn't buy those.

GARY. Someone probably gave them to him.

MARY-ELLEN. Now? No. It's too late for that.

GARY. Why –

MARY-ELLEN. Is he seeing someone?

GARY. Who?

MARY-ELLEN. A woman?

GARY. No.

MARY-ELLEN. How do you know?

GARY. His wife has been dead two months.

MARY-ELLEN. So.

GARY. So, he's not that kind of man.

MARY-ELLEN. He's in mourning.

GARY. I know –

MARY-ELLEN. People do things. I mean, what about me. I'm not the kind person that sleeps for forty-eight hours at a time, mumbles, and plucks out both eyebrows, but I did that when I lost my brother.

GARY. You did?

MARY-ELLEN. Walter could be filling his emptiness with a woman.

GARY. He worshipped Margaret.

MARY-ELLEN. So?

GARY. No woman could ever fill her shoes.

MARY-ELLEN. Well, she doesn't have to fill Margaret's shoes, Gary. She just has to be a warm body.

GARY. He wouldn't do that.

MARY-ELLEN. How do you know?

GARY. Let's go.

MARY-ELLEN. Something's different.

GARY. It's none of our business.

MARY-ELLEN. What?

GARY. I don't want to talk about this.

MARY-ELLEN. Gary.

GARY. I don't want to talk about it.

MARY-ELLEN. He's your best friend.

GARY. So was she.

(He exits.)

(She continues to look around.)

(And follows him out.)

Scene Eleven

(Wells living room)

*(**BAO** examines the room. He picks up various items: A baby picture. Barbie doll that is still on shelf. A vase. A bowling trophy. Fake fruit. [He smells it. Then bangs a fake apple on a table. Wood?] He wanders over to a shelf full of books and photo albums.)*

(He takes one of the albums and sits on the couch, looking through it.)

*(**WALTER** enters.)*

WALTER. What are you doing?

BAO. I'm just looking.

WALTER. Stop.

BAO. I just –

WALTER. Put that down please.

*(**BAO** closes the album. Looks at his watch.)*

BAO. I'm sorry, I didn't know it was so late –

WALTER. This isn't working for me.

BAO. It is a beautiful family.

*(**WALTER** takes the albums from him.)*

I have only one photo of my family.

WALTER. Well, I'm sorry to hear that.

*(**WALTER** puts the albums back on the shelf. Rearranges the things **BAO** moved, exactly as they were.)*

BAO. What is that fruit for?

WALTER. Decoration.

BAO. But you can't eat it –

WALTER. Listen, I'm not comfortable with you going through my things.

BAO. I was just looking –

WALTER. Margaret was very particular about her decorations. I don't want you touching them –

BAO. I just looked –

WALTER. Don't touch anything.

BAO. OK –

WALTER. Is this what you do when you come here? Sneak through my life?

BAO. No.

(**WALTER** *just looks at him.*)

No. I promise.

WALTER. This was a bad idea. Give me the key.

BAO. No.

WALTER. I wasn't thinking clearly –

BAO. No. I'm sorry. I'm sorry. I won't look at your pictures again. I promise. I just want to see your family.

WALTER. Why?

BAO. I won't look again. I promise. I'm sorry. I won't touch anything.

(**BAO** *heads for the door.*)

WALTER. What were you looking for?

BAO. Nothing.

WALTER. Money?

BAO. No.

(*silence*)

No. I won't do it again. I promise. I'm sorry.

WALTER. Where do you live?

(**BAO** *keeps walking for the door.*)

BAO. I'm sorry.

WALTER. Where do you live?

BAO. Saigon.

WALTER. I mean here in Garden Grove.

BAO. I live with my cousin.

WALTER. Where?

BAO. Bixby Avenue.

WALTER. I assume you take the bus now?

> (**BAO** *stops.*)

BAO. Yes.

WALTER. Do you have a job?

BAO. Yes.

WALTER. Where?

BAO. I work at night.

WALTER. Where?

BAO. A bakery. My cousin's friend –

WALTER. I thought you said you were a doctor.

BAO. I am.

> (*silence*)

There is soup in the kitchen.

> (**BAO** *exits.*)

> (**WALTER** *adjusts the decorations. Again.*)

Scene Twelve

(Wells Living Room)

(**WALTER**, **GARY**, **MARY-ELLEN** *sit watching television. A laugh track can be heard.*)

(**GARY** *and* **MARY-ELLEN** *laugh.*)

(**WALTER** *is distracted.*)

GARY. Walter loves this show. Don't you, Walter.

MARY-ELLEN. I just think it's hysterical.

GARY. Funny. Huh?

(They both look at him.)

Lifts the old spirits, doesn't it?

(They keep looking at him.)

(**WALTER** *pushes a smile.*)

(They return their attention to the TV.)

MARY-ELLEN. I'd date that Tim Conway in a heartbeat if he wasn't so short.

(They keep watching.)

MARY-ELLEN. He is fun.

GARY. How do you know he'd date you?

MARY-ELLEN. What are you saying?

GARY. Nothing, I just –

MARY-ELLEN. I'm not good enough for Tim Conway?

GARY. I just find it a bit presumptuous of you to assume he would date you just because you want to date him.

MARY-ELLEN. Worked on you.

GARY. Well –

MARY-ELLEN. Clearly, I'm irresistible.

GARY. I'm not famous.

MARY-ELLEN. So you can't speak for a famous person, can you. You don't know what famous people would or wouldn't do.

GARY. I guess not –

MARY-ELLEN. But, they want the same things we do, Gary.

GARY. Maybe, but –

MARY-ELLEN. They want to have a good time and have wild sex and eat good food. Just because I'm not a millionaire doesn't mean Tim Conway wouldn't want to spend time with me. Take me to dinner. Show me the town.

GARY. Maybe –

MARY-ELLEN. Besides, it would be *me* turning him down remember. I wouldn't want to lead him on because I just don't see myself in a long-term serious relationship with a terribly short man.

GARY. What –

MARY-ELLEN. It's bad for the back, all that leaning down. And I like high heels. I'd choose the heels over him. I like to be honest up front.

(**GARY** *just looks at her.*)

It's only fair. Right, Walter?

GARY. What if I wanted to date Carol Burnett?

MARY-ELLEN. Oh, please.

GARY. What?

MARY-ELLEN. She'd never date you.

GARY. Why not?

MARY-ELLEN. Why would she drive all the way down here, from Hollywood, to have a date with you?

GARY. Same reason Tim Conway would come down see you.

MARY-ELLEN. No.

GARY. Why not?

MARY-ELLEN. She could have anyone. Tim Conway, on the other hand, being short as he is, and balding, has fewer options.

(**GARY** *gets up.*)

GARY. So what's wrong with me?

MARY-ELLEN. Nothing.

GARY. I'm not short.

MARY-ELLEN. I know.

GARY. I have my hair.

MARY-ELLEN. Mostly.

GARY. So why wouldn't someone come down to have date with me?

MARY-ELLEN. What do you have to offer?

GARY. A good time.

MARY-ELLEN. Marriage?

(silence)

GARY. Well, would they come for Walter?

MARY-ELLEN. Of course.

GARY. Why?

MARY-ELLEN. He's handsome, kind, and grieving.

GARY. He's practically comatose. No offense, Walter.

MARY-ELLEN. Women flock to guys like this.

GARY. Why?

MARY-ELLEN. Look at him. Needy. Hurt. Sad.

GARY. What wrong with me?

MARY-ELLEN. You are a whole man. Happy, complete. Not a care in the world.

(GARY looks at WALTER. WALTER is oblivious; he scratches his head.)

GARY. This logic is beyond me.

(He exits to the kitchen.)

MARY-ELLEN. No offense, Walter.

(Laugh track from the TV)

I just don't want Gary to take me for granted. That I don't have other suitors. I have to keep him on his toes. Worried and a bit confused.

(WALTER keeps his eyes on the TV)

You know what I mean?

(More laugh track.)

WALTER. I'm sorry, did you say something?

MARY-ELLEN. Oh nothing. It doesn't matter.

(More laugh track.)

Scene Thirteen

(Wells living room)

(Morning)

(WALTER *is still on the couch. He's been awake all night.)*

(BAO *enters with two loaves of bread.)*

BAO. Oh. You're still here. I'm sorry.

(BAO *begins to turn to exit, remembers the bread and sets it on a coffee table.)*

I'm sorry. This is for you. I'll go –

WALTER. Is that from where you work?

BAO. Yes.

WALTER. There's some coffee in the kitchen. If you want.

(silence)

Cups are in the cabinet.

(BAO *looks at* **WALTER.***)*

WALTER. What?

BAO. I can open the cabinet? *Touch* the cup?

(WALTER *just looks at him.)*

WALTER. Yes.

(BAO *exits to the kitchen. Returns with the pot.)*

(He refills **WALTER***'s cup and pours a cup for himself.)*

WALTER. What do you do here all day?

BAO. Dance.

WALTER. Seriously.

(BAO *takes the pot to the kitchen and returns with a plate of fruit.)*

(WALTER *just looks at* **BAO.***)*

(They sit there. Long silence. Awkward. Drinking coffee.)

(Finally.)

BAO. This is a very beautiful house. The kitchen. The bath-room. Very modern.

WALTER. It's got it all.

BAO. I see houses like this on television in Vietnam. I thought they were not true. Not real life.

(silence)

This is real.

(silence)

(**WALTER** *finally looks at his watch.*)

WALTER. I have to get to work.

(He stands up.)

(Long silence.)

I really think this is very unhealthy. This. Arrangement.

(silence)

Every time I think about…every time I look at you, I just…

(silence)

Why? Why me?

BAO. Then we are thinking the same thing.

(silence)

WALTER. What kind of doctor are you? You're not a shrink, are you?

BAO. Pediatrician.

(**WALTER** *nods.*)

WALTER. Well.

(silence)

I don't know what to do.

(silence)

I just don't know what to do anymore. About anything.

BAO. You want to kill me?

WALTER. No.

BAO. I will let you.

WALTER. No.

BAO. Please.

WALTER. I would never do that.

(*silence*)

BAO. OK.

(*silence*)

I will make more food for you.

(*silence*)

WALTER. If you're going to dance, please just keep your clothes on. I have neighbors.

BAO. I will try.

(**WALTER** *exits.*)

(**BAO** *looks around the house, then looks at the large family photo on the wall.*)

(*He sings a Vietnamese lullaby.*)

(*He takes the one small family photo he has from his wallet, and adds it to the large Wells family photo.*)

(*He takes fruit from his bag, and incense, and adds it to the make-shift altar.*)

(*He lights the incense, and sets them up below the photos.*)

(*He prays.*)

Scene Fourteen

(Outside the church.)

(GARY *and* **WALTER)**

(GARY *wears his sunglasses.)*

GARY. That was, by far, the worst sermon I have ever given.

WALTER. What language were you speaking?

GARY. I don't know.

WALTER. Everything you said ended with a K or a P.

(GARY holds his head.)

WALTER. "Jesusk." "Let us prayp."
(sings) "Amen....K"

GARY. Mary-Ellen made Sangria last night and I have no idea what was in it. I did see a bottle of Cold Duck and a bottle of Ripple on her kitchen counter. Which should have warned me.

WALTER. You think?

GARY. It just went down so easy.

WALTER. What are you two, eighteen?

GARY. And she made this egg salad dip...

(He gives a slight heave.)

Can't think about that....But. It was fun. Man. Mary-Ellen was wearing a wig when we went to bed. I woke up with it on my head. I have no idea how it got there. She is a good time, that woman. A very good time.

WALTER. You're green.

GARY. It's nice to see you back here.

WALTER. I didn't come for your riveting sermons.

GARY. We've missed you –

WALTER. Or the Go*p* talk.

GARY. Sunday's just not the same without Walter Wells.

WALTER. Well, some old habits are hard to break.

GARY. See? You missed the church.

WALTER. I missed your coffee and doughnuts.

GARY. Whatever it takes.

(silence)

WALTER. I gotta get home...

GARY. Did you meet someone?

WALTER. What?

GARY. Have you met someone?

WALTER. Who?

GARY. A woman.

WALTER. What?

GARY. It's Mary-Ellen. She thinks you met someone. I told her, it was impossible.

WALTER. It is impossible.

(silence)

That's the last thing on my mind.

GARY. That's exactly what I said.

WALTER. Where'd she get that idea?

GARY. Your house is clean.

WALTER. I can't keep a clean house?

GARY. She said that she, not me –

WALTER. This Women's Movement really galls me...Who says a man won't clean his own house?

GARY. I clean my own house.

WALTER. You have a housekeeper.

GARY. Not every week –

WALTER. What else did she say?

GARY. You have fresh flowers.

WALTER. People sent them to me.

GARY. That what I said.

WALTER. What if they didn't? A *man* can't buy fresh flowers for himself?

GARY. I don't know –

WALTER. What does it matter to you what I have in my house? Or who?

GARY. It doesn't.

WALTER. Then why are you asking about it?

GARY. I'm just, just checking in.

WALTER. Why?

GARY. Well. You barely leave your house. You don't call. You work until all hours of the night. This is the first Sunday you've been here –

WALTER. So?

GARY. I'm worried about you.

WALTER. That is the worse part of this whole thing. Suddenly everyone treats me like I'm their pet that needs to be watched and cared for.

GARY. We're your friends.

WALTER. So stop treating me like a child. Stop watching everything I do.

GARY. I asked one question –

WALTER. It was a shitty question.

GARY. Sorry –

WALTER. And ring the doorbell when you come to my house. You didn't just let yourself in when Margaret and the kids were around, why would you do that now?

GARY. I shouldn't have asked. I'm sorry.

WALTER. I'm surrounded by her clothes. Her perfume. Her shampoo, every time I take a shower. Sometimes I open the bottle and just stand there, smelling it. For hours. I can't move.

(silence)

She's every place I look. She's all over the house –

GARY. I am sorry. I'm no good at this –

WALTER. Lisa and Danny are in every corner. Their toys. Their shoes. Sitting next to Margaret's. Waiting for them to come home. I can still hear them in the house…Then I start thinking of their last moments.

Were they afraid? Did they call for me? Were they
afraid and I wasn't there?...Covered in blood...And I
can't fucking move.

GARY. I'm sorry.

WALTER. Didn't you love her? The kids? –

GARY. Of course I did. Of course.

(silence)

I would have married Margaret if you hadn't gotten to
her first.

WALTER. You don't marry.

GARY. Well, I would have married her. She was the smartest,
sexiest, funniest woman in the room. Killer combo.

(silence)

Everyone was jealous of your family. Even me.

WALTER. Then how could you think I could replace her?

GARY. I drank a gallon of alcohol last night. I'm clearly not
thinking straight. Mary-Ellen just gets me all confused.
The woman overwhelms me. However –

(A small belch/heave.)

Oh god. That egg salad's a killer.

(He pushes back the heave.)

However. I do think it is important to stake. To state.
Without offending you. That if you do feel the need to
find a woman, to ease the pain you're going through
right now, no one would judge you for it. And I mean,
no one.

WALTER. Please –

GARY. God is merciful –

WALTER. Don't start.

GARY. I just want you to know that.

WALTER. OK.

GARY. Everyone wants you to be happy –

(Small heave.)

GARY. *(cont.)* Whatever it takes.

> *(Another heave.)*

We just want you to be happy again.

> *(Another heave.)*

Excuse me.

> *(He rushes off the stage to vomit.)*

> (**WALTER** *puts on his sunglasses, and slowly exits.*)

Scene Fifteen

(Evening)

(Wells living room)

*(**BAO** studies a checkerboard.)*

*(**WALTER** enters with two plates of cake.)*

WALTER. One of the neighbors brought this by. This stuff just keeps coming. It's lemon something, I think.

(He sits down. Waits.)

*(**BAO** takes a bite of cake.)*

BAO. Good. I like lemon.

*(**BAO** studies the board a moment longer, then makes a move that takes three of **WALTER**'s pieces.)*

*(**WALTER** just looks at him.)*

It's an easy game.

*(**WALTER** studies the board.)*

WALTER. Where, where did you study to be a doctor?

BAO. Saigon.

WALTER. Your English is very good.

BAO. No. No. My French is much better.

WALTER. You speak French?

BAO. Yes. You?

WALTER. No. I'm not that great with languages. Four letter words, curse words, yes, but not foreign ones.

BAO. What?

WALTER. Swear words?…"Fuck." "Shit." "Goddamn it." "Asshole." "Motherfucking cocksucker ding dong."

*(**BAO** nods, unsure.)*

Never mind.

*(**WALTER** makes a move on the checkerboard.)*

*(**BAO** studies the board.)*

WALTER. *(cont.)* I've never been out of the country. Of course, I was too old to be drafted for Vietnam. I had a cousin who went. He came back crazy.

(silence)

I wonder if I would have been one of those guys to run off to Canada.

(silence)

Probably not. I'm not really a rule-breaker. I generally pay my taxes and do what I'm supposed to do. For better or worse.

(silence)

I have become my father.

(**BAO** *is still trying to figure out his next move.*)

What about your folks?

BAO. What?

WALTER. Your parents?

BAO. They are dead.

WALTER. Recently?

BAO. Seven years.

WALTER. What happened?

BAO. A bomb on their village.

(silence)

WALTER. American?

BAO. Yes.

(**BAO** *makes a move on the board. Takes another of* **WALTER**'s *pieces.*)

WALTER. That must have been terrible.

BAO. Yes.

WALTER. And your kids? Your wife?

(silence)

BAO. You want more coffee?

WALTER. Oh. No. Thank you. You make it strong.

BAO. Too strong?

WALTER. No. It's good.

(**BAO** *checks his watch.*)

BAO. I have to go to work now.

WALTER. But we haven't finished the game.

BAO. I don't want to be late. The bakery is very strict.

WALTER. Oh. OK.

BAO. Thank you for your hospitality, Mr. Wells.

WALTER. My name is Walter.

BAO. I know.

WALTER. You can call me Walter.

BAO. I am not comfortable with calling you by your first name.

WALTER. Why not?

BAO. We are not friends. Thank you for the easy game. And the cake. I appreciate that.

WALTER. I'll save the game. We can finish it tomorrow –

BAO. Good-bye, Mr. Wells.

WALTER. See you tomorrow? You're coming tomorrow, right?

BAO. Yes.

(**WALTER** *nods. Sitting alone under that large family portrait.*)

(**BAO** *exits.*)

(**WALTER** *is still nodding as he listens to the front door close.*)

End of Act 1

ACT 2

Scene One

(Golf course. Bright, sunny day.)

(WALTER and GARY enter in golf clothes, golf clubs in hand. They are looking around.)

(They look into the sun, the distance.)

(Keep waiting.)

(They keep looking.)

(Finally MARY-ELLEN enters, out of breath.)

MARY-ELLEN. I think a raccoon got it. Dammit.

GARY. Why would a raccoon take your golf ball?

MARY-ELLEN. Have you ever seen the hands on a raccoon?

GARY. Yes.

MARY-ELLEN. They are the perfect size to fit around a golf ball. It would be a little treasure in those hands.

GARY. A treasure for what?

MARY-ELLEN. I don't know how raccoons thinks, Gary. I'm not a raccoon mind-reader. I just know they have crafty little hands.

GARY. You shouldn't have hit it so far out there.

MARY-ELLEN. I don't know my own strength.

WALTER. I watched one eat a piece of pepperoni pizza once.

MARY-ELLEN. They're no-good scavenging thieves. Out playing god-knows-what with my ball, while I'm walking the ends of the earth looking for it. Jerks. Let's get a drink.

GARY. We still have one more hole.

MARY-ELLEN. I'm done.

GARY. You can't be.

MARY-ELLEN. I have no ball.

GARY. This isn't about you. We finally, finally get Walter out of the house, into some fresh air –

MARY-ELLEN. Walter? Do you want to keep playing?

WALTER. No.

GARY. Why not?

WALTER. You won.

GARY. But we didn't finish.

MARY-ELLEN. C'mon, Walter swings like a girl. And my ball was accosted by rodents. You won the game, Gary.

GARY. How can I win if we only played eight holes?

WALTER. I don't swing like a girl –

GARY. That's no fun.

MARY-ELLEN. I'll buy you a trophy.

GARY. I don't want a trophy. I just want to play one decent game of golf.

MARY-ELLEN. Then why'd you ask us?

WALTER. I play a decent game –

GARY. This is about Walter. His mental state. I think you've improved greatly –

WALTER. Leave my mental state out of it.

MARY-ELLEN. Walter's mental state needs rigourous activity, joy, and exhaustion. Not this tedious geezer game.

GARY. This is very relaxing.

MARY-ELLEN. We're going to go exhaust our sorrows with a strong, beautiful drink. Like normal people on a Saturday.

GARY. Will you please just let me finish?

MARY-ELLEN. You finish the game and then come tell us about it.

GARY. It's no fun to tell someone you got a hole-in-one if no one was there to see it.

MARY-ELLEN. Are you going to get a hole-in-one?

GARY. I might.

WALTER. I'll buy you a drink if you do.

GARY. See, no one will believe me.

MARY-ELLEN. You're a man of God, Gary. Lying is a sin.

GARY. I guess –

MARY-ELLEN. And if you see that goddamn raccoon with my ball, whack him on the head, will you? That's much better than a hole-in-one.

GARY. How?

MARY-ELLEN. I'll get my damn ball back.

(**WALTER** *and* **MARY-ELLEN** *exit.*)

(**GARY**, *confused, exits in the opposite direction.*)

Scene Two

(Outside patio)

(WALTER and MARY-ELLEN sit with their faces in the sun, Bloody Marys in hand.)

MARY-ELLEN. What a day.

WALTER. Yep.

MARY-ELLEN. You couldn't pay me to live in Michigan again. I mean, look at us, it's November for Christ's sake.

WALTER. Is that where you're from?

MARY-ELLEN. Yeah. I got a ride out of Lansing at eighteen, and I haven't looked back. You?

WALTER. Wisconsin.

MARY-ELLEN. Really?

(She taps his drink with hers.)

MARY-ELLEN. Go cheeseheads.

WALTER. I came out here for college.

MARY-ELLEN. Yeah?

WALTER. Graduated. Then met Margaret. Got married. Etc.

MARY-ELLEN. I should have done that. Instead, I spent my youth chasing boys with surfboards.

WALTER. That's fun.

MARY-ELLEN. It was. But now I'm spending middle-age answering telephones for angry men with law degrees, who ask me to get their coffee. Not fun.

WALTER. Margaret wanted a career.

MARY-ELLEN. Grass is always greener.

WALTER. Yep.

MARY-ELLEN. Tell me something. Why do you think Gary is still a bachelor? You think there's something wrong with him?

WALTER. No.

MARY-ELLEN. Has he ever asked a woman to marry him?

WALTER. No.

MARY-ELLEN. Is he a homosexual? Am I dating a homosexual?

WALTER. No.

MARY-ELLEN. Does he have a checkered past?

(**WALTER** *just looks at her.*)

WALTER. No.

MARY-ELLEN. Well, that can be a very sexy quality. Rugged. Incarcerated.

WALTER. He's just afraid to make a commitment.

MARY-ELLEN. Why?

WALTER. I have no idea.

MARY-ELLEN. Is no girl good enough?

WALTER. I have no idea.

MARY-ELLEN. Well, maybe we're perfect for each other. I'm horrible at marriage. And I'm not sure I can have kids. My time may have passed for that. So, what you see now is what you get. In all my glory.

(*They both take a drink.*)

There's a slight age difference between Gary and I. If you hadn't noticed.

WALTER. No. I hadn't.

MARY-ELLEN. You are kind, Walter Wells.

(*silence*)

Would you marry again?

(*silence*)

I'm sure the women are already lined up. Good man like you.

WALTER. I'm not seeing anyone, Mary-Ellen. Since I hear you're wondering.

MARY-ELLEN. Well –

WALTER. They can line up all they want.

MARY-ELLEN. Well, there's something going on in your house.

WALTER. Like what?

MARY-ELLEN. You tell me.

WALTER. You're too nosy.

MARY-ELLEN. Someone is taking care of you.

WALTER. Taking care of me?

MARY-ELLEN. Someone's in your house. You can't fool me.

WALTER. I'm not trying to fool you.

MARY-ELLEN. Walter. Please.

WALTER. What?

MARY-ELLEN. I'm a very perceptive person. I'm border-line psychic. Don't insult me.

(silence)

WALTER. I sometimes spend time with Bao Ngo.

MARY-ELLEN. Who?

WALTER. Bao Ngo. The man, the man who was driving the car that killed Margaret and Danny and Lisa.

(silence)

MARY-ELLEN. You're kidding?

WALTER. No.

MARY-ELLEN. Why?

WALTER. I have no idea.

MARY-ELLEN. How did that start?

WALTER. Well –

MARY-ELLEN. Spend time doing what?

WALTER. He came to the store and he had bandages on his wrists and he wanted to do something to make me feel better and to appease himself maybe, I don't know, then he was down on his knees, begging, and…So…he started coming to my house and cooking food for me everyday. It's the only thing I can eat right now, which is weird…everything else reminds me of Margaret. And now sometimes we just sit there. Saying nothing. Staring at the walls. Sometimes we play a game or watch TV.

MARY-ELLEN. Is that fun?

WALTER. Not particularly.

MARY-ELLEN. What is it?

WALTER. It's just what it is.

MARY-ELLEN. That's weird, Walter.

WALTER. I know.

MARY-ELLEN. So, what, are you friends?

WALTER. No.

MARY-ELLEN. What are you?

WALTER. I have no idea.

> *(silence)*

> But he's the one person that isn't constantly trying to cheer me up. Or comfort me. I don't have to explain anything. He's perfectly fine with just sitting there.

> *(silence)*

> I still want to hit him sometimes. Just punch him in the face. I don't. So we just sit there. I think he's pretty messed up.

> *(silence)*

> Maybe he wants to hit me.

MARY-ELLEN. I swear to God, this is the last thing I would have guessed was going on at your house. I thought for sure you had that prissy Carol Martin coming over.

WALTER. No.

MARY-ELLEN. You know, she lets her dog poop on my yard?

WALTER. How do you know it's her dog?

MARY-ELLEN. Oh, I know. That's cocker spaniel shit. It's not my fault her husband looks at me in my yard when I'm sun-bathing.

WALTER. Don't tell Gary. About Bao.

MARY-ELLEN. Why not?

WALTER. It doesn't concern him.

MARY-ELLEN. He cares about you –

WALTER. It's my business, Mary-Ellen.

MARY-ELLEN. Are you coming over for Thanksgiving? You can bring your new friend as your date –

WALTER. I mean it.

MARY-ELLEN. OK. Are you coming for –

WALTER. No.

MARY-ELLEN. Why not?

WALTER. I can't.

MARY-ELLEN. Did Gary say something about my cooking?

WALTER. No.

MARY-ELLEN. Do I over-salt? Is that what he said?

WALTER. I don't want to be the drunk man crying into the tablecloth. Ruining everyone else's day. Really.

MARY-ELLEN. You can cry all you want. No one will care.

WALTER. I will.

MARY-ELLEN. You cannot sit home alone on Thanksgiving.

WALTER. Yes I can.

MARY-ELLEN. No you can't.

WALTER. Watch me.

MARY-ELLEN. It's un-American.

    *(***GARY** *enters.)*

GARY. I got a hole-in-one.

MARY-ELLEN. Bull shit.

WALTER. I don't believe it.

GARY. I did. I got a hole-in-one.

MARY-ELLEN. No.

GARY. I swear to God above. On my own personal Bible. Walter has to buy me a drink.

MARY-ELLEN. Walter isn't coming for Thanksgiving.

GARY. What?

MARY-ELLEN. He wants to stay home alone.

GARY. That's impossible.

    (to **WALTER***)*

You can't do that.

WALTER. I'm not going to put Christmas lights on my house this year either.

GARY. *(gasp)* No. Please. Yours is the best on the block.

MARY-ELLEN. Walter. Don't say that.

WALTER. And no Christmas tree.

MARY-ELLEN & GARY. *(gasp)* No.

GARY. *(gasp)* Walter. Please.

MARY-ELLEN. You can't just give up.

GARY. Everyone will be so disappointed.

WALTER. I don't care.

> (**WALTER** *gets up, cheerful.*)

> Who wants a drink?

> (**MARY-ELLEN** *and* **GARY** *watch him exit, then follow, concerned.*)

> *(Finally.)*

MARY-ELLEN. You did not get a hole-in-one.

GARY. Yes I did.

Scene Three

(Wells living room)

*(**BAO** and **WALTER** sit watching a football game.)*

*(**WALTER** claps.)*

WALTER. Oh yeah. Nice one.

(More clapping.)

WALTER. That's the way we do it. OK. Now we're getting somewhere.

BAO. What?

WALTER. That was a perfect block. Great run. Beautiful play.

BAO. Oh.

(They watch the game.)

WALTER. See, now, I think this is going to be a pass play.

(They watch, watch…)

WALTER. Oh! Damn it! C'mon!

BAO. What?

WALTER. Overthrew the receiver!

BAO. Oh.

WALTER. Jesus Christ.

(A TV commercial plays offstage.)

*(**WALTER** gets up.)*

You want another beer?

BAO. Yes. Please.

WALTER. Hungry?

BAO. No. Thank you.

WALTER. Chips?

BAO. No. Thank you –

WALTER. I'll get chips.

(He exits.)

*(**BAO** looks around the room.)*

*(**WALTER** returns with two beers. Chips, dip.)*

WALTER. *(cont.)* I appreciate you coming over. I thought maybe someone might have asked you to come have turkey dinner with them.

BAO. No.

WALTER. Well. That's too bad. It's a pretty great meal.

*(He hands **BAO** the beer.)*

WALTER. Maybe next year.

BAO. Maybe.

*(**WALTER** sits beside him.)*

WALTER. I just decided…I'm just going to let the day pass, you know. If I just let it go by, it won't be a holiday, right? Just any old day.

BAO. Yes.

WALTER. Any old day. And then tomorrow, it's done. Right?

BAO. Right.

(silence)

(They watch another TV commercial.)

(They continue to watch the commercial.)

WALTER. That is a good looking car.

BAO. Yes.

WALTER. My sister bought one of those.

BAO. Really?

WALTER. Yeah.

(silence)

Hers has vinyl seats.

BAO. Oh.

(silence)

What is vinyl?

WALTER. It's kinda like leather but cheaper. Good if you have kids. Easy clean up.

(silence)

WALTER. *(cont.)* It can get hot though. In the sun. Kids used to complain it burned their legs.

(silence)

Yeah.

(silence)

You like it here?

BAO. Where?

WALTER. America. California.

BAO. It doesn't matter.

WALTER. What do you mean?

BAO. It's the same.

(silence)

Same.

(silence)

WALTER. It'll get better.

(silence)

Couldn't get any worse, right?

BAO. That's what I thought when I was leaving Vietnam.

(silence)

It got worse.

WALTER. Do you think you'll ever go back?

BAO. You still want me to go back?

WALTER. No – That wasn't my question –

BAO. I will not go back. No.

WALTER. What happened to your wife, your kids?

BAO. Gone.

WALTER. How?

BAO. Just gone.

WALTER. How?

(silence)

WALTER. How?

BAO. When Saigon was falling, my wife wouldn't leave. She wouldn't let me take my son. Or my daughter.

WALTER. Why not?

BAO. She didn't want to leave home.

WALTER. But you left?

BAO. I had to. I had American friends. They were my patients. I would have been killed. I begged her to come with me...It was very chaotic that day. Loud. People were pushing on each other. Yelling. And one minute I'm yelling for her to come with me, grabbing for my children, and the next I'm leaving alone.

(silence)

She thought maybe it would be OK with the communists. She loved Vietnam. She wanted to stay.

(silence)

She was a famous singer. Stubborn.

(silence)

Three days after that. They were killed.

WALTER. Shot?

BAO. No. My wife tried to get to her parents house. Out in the countryside. And they ran across a land mine.

WALTER. Jesus.

(silence)

How did you find out?

BAO. One of my friends sent me a letter. I got it when I was in that Camp, Camp Pendleton.

(silence)

And three months later, I think, ok, ok, I will try and make a better life here. I will pull myself up. I will try. I will drive a car. I will go to the ocean. I will go see how beautiful California is. And I kill your family on that day.

(silence)

BAO. *(cont.)* So. I'm not sure how I like America. It doesn't matter.

(*silence*)

There is nothing but death everywhere I go.

WALTER. It won't be like that forever.

BAO. How do you know?

WALTER. You're alive.

BAO. So?

WALTER. It will get better. It has to, right?

BAO. Who says?

WALTER. It just does.

BAO. Why?

WALTER. Because it has to. It just has to.

BAO. I will still go to hell. For what I've done.

WALTER. Please –

BAO. You will still hate me for what I've done.

(*silence*)

WALTER. You don't know that.

BAO. I will still have no family. No home.

WALTER. You could start again.

BAO. No.

WALTER. Maybe.

BAO. I am a ghost now.

WALTER. Don't be so dramatic.

BAO. I am not being dramatic!

(*silence*)

You think that all of life is like this? So easy? You think all people have this nice TV? This furniture? This what do you call it…this shack carpeting?

WALTER. Shag –

BAO. Not everyone is rich.

WALTER. I'm not rich –

BAO. This is rich –

WALTER. No. It's not.

BAO. In Vietnam, this is rich. You don't understand –

WALTER. I'm not going to apologize for my house, my life, alright. And it's not so easy –

BAO. I have seen children burned to their bones. Their faces gone…Their houses nothing but rocks on the ground. Their families destroyed…Not everything gets better. Some things get worse.

WALTER. Maybe.

BAO. Vietnam gets worse by the day.

WALTER. Maybe.

BAO. My life gets only worse.

WALTER. That could change –

BAO. I'm not waiting for it to change. Or get better. I want it to end.

WALTER. You're alive, aren't you?

BAO. I don't care.

WALTER. You better start caring, asshole, because others died when you got to live. My family. Your family.

(*silence*)

You're standing here alive and breathing, while they are all dead in the ground.

BAO. I wish it was me.

(*silence*)

My heart is dead. I'm a ghost now.

(**WALTER** *punches him in the arm.*)

WALTER. That hurt?

BAO. Yes.

WALTER. Then you're not a ghost.

(*silence*)

You like onion dip?

BAO. What?

WALTER. Do you like onion dip?

BAO. I don't know.

WALTER. Try it. Dip that chip in there.

BAO. No.

WALTER. Dip it.

BAO. No.

WALTER. Dip it! I made it. C'mon. The fourth quarter has started.

(**BAO** *tries the dip.*)

WALTER. Well?

BAO. It's good.

WALTER. Ghosts can't enjoy onion dip, can they?

(**WALTER** *tries it.*)

That is delicious.

(**WALTER** *turns up the volume on the TV.*)

(*He watches the game.*)

(*Claps his hands.*)

Nice! Yeah!

(*More clapping.*)

That was a beautiful play. That's what they get paid the big bucks for.

(*They watch.*)

See?

(*More clapping.*)

Things get better.

Scene Four

(Wells Appliance)

(The phone rings.)

*(****WALTER*** *enters with a cup of coffee.)*

(He looks at the phone but doesn't answer it.)

(He stands staring at it.)

(Finally.)

WALTER. Seasons Greetings. Wells Appliance. Oh hello Bill. I'm, I'm well, thank you. Uh huh….Yeah. Yeah. Great. The dryer too? Great. That's a nice gift. Yeah. I think she'll love it…You want me to put a big Christmas bow on that? Uh huh. Sure. Sure. We can do that. Wonderful… Of course I remember him, sure…How old is he now?…Wow…Uh huh…Yeah, swimming is a great sport. He did? How fast did he swim it?… You're kidding?…Wow. That is fast…Sounds like you got yourself the next Mark Spitz…Uh huh. Uh huh. Listen, I've, I've got another customer waiting on me, but I'll be sure to get that order ready for you…OK then. Will do. You too. Bye. Bye.

(He hangs up.)

(Stares at the phone.)

(Takes it off the hook.)

Scene Five

(Christmas.)

(Vietnamese music plays. Female singer.)

(Wells living room.)

(BAO *and* **WALTER** *enter from the sliding door with plates of steak and baked potatoes.)*

WALTER. Next year you'll be invited to a big family gathering somewhere. I'm sure of it.

BAO. We'll see.

*(**BAO** sits on the couch. **WALTER** beside him.)*

WALTER. How's the steak? Is it OK?

*(**BAO** was waiting for **WALTER** to eat, but tastes it.)*

BAO. Good.

(silence)

WALTER. Nice music.

BAO. I told you. Famous in Vietnam.

(silence)

BAO. My wife was very beautiful. I like these potatoes.

WALTER. Really? I wasn't sure if I made them right.

BAO. Good.

WALTER. You gotta have potatoes with steak, right?

BAO. You do?

WALTER. Trust me.

(They keep eating.)

WALTER. What'd she look like?

BAO. My wife?

WALTER. Yeah.

BAO. Long hair. Very serious eyes. Stubborn.

*(**BAO** takes his family photo from his wallet, and hands it to **WALTER**.)*

My children have the same eyes.

(**WALTER** *nods, shaken.*)

(**WALTER** *finally hands him back the photo and* **BAO** *returns it to his wallet.*)

(*silence*)

BAO. (*cont.*) This is a very good dinner.

WALTER. You want to watch TV? The news is on –

BAO. I don't want to watch the news.

WALTER. Me either. Why spoil the dinner, right?

BAO. I like this steak.

WALTER. It's not too rare, is it –

BAO. No –

WALTER. It's really easy. You just throw it on the grill –

MARY-ELLEN. (*offstage*) "Hark the herald angels sing"…

> (**MARY-ELLEN** *and* **GARY** *enter with a pitcher of eggnog, and a small Christmas tree.*)

GARY. "Glory to the new-born king."

MARY-ELLEN & GARY. "Peace on Earth, and Mercy Mild, God and Sinners, Reconciled, Joyfull all ye…"

WALTER. Do you mind?

GARY. What?

WALTER. Doorbell?

MARY-ELLEN. It's Christmas.

> (**GARY** *and* **MARY-ELLEN** *stare at* **BAO**.)

GARY. I'm Gary.

MARY-ELLEN. Mary-Ellen.

> (**WALTER** *gets up and turns off the music.*)

BAO. Bao.

MARY-ELLEN. Merry Christmas.

GARY. And how do you know Walter?

MARY-ELLEN. Gary –

GARY. Oh. Right. OK.

> (*silence*)

GARY. Welcome!

MARY-ELLEN. Who would like eggnog?

WALTER. I really wish you all would –

MARY-ELLEN. I don't want to hear it. This is a special day and I won't have you over here sulking.

WALTER. I'm not sulking.

(**MARY-ELLEN** *enters into the kitchen.*)

GARY. Where do you want this tree?

WALTER. Outside.

GARY. I'll put it in the corner here. Look, we already strung the lights on it and hung some ornaments. It's all set.

(*He plugs the lights in.*)

There we go. See? Look at that. Instant Christmas.

(*He looks over their dinner.*)

Nice looking steak. What else you got there? Potatoes –

WALTER. I'm really not in the mood for all this, Gary.

GARY. I'm starving.

WALTER. I mean it –

GARY. She cooked a goose, and I don't know what was inside it. A shoe maybe –

(**MARY-ELLEN** *returns with glasses.*)

MARY-ELLEN. Here we are.

GARY. Delicious eggnog!

(*She takes in the tree.*)

MARY-ELLEN. Oh, would you look at that. Lovely. The party has begun.

WALTER. I don't want a party.

MARY-ELLEN. Don't be silly.

(**GARY** *and* **MARY-ELLEN** *serve up the nog.*)

MARY-ELLEN. Eggnog, Bao?

BAO. OK.

GARY. Have you had it before?

BAO. No.

GARY. American tradition. Mary-Ellen puts a little more booze there than most, but, you, you get the idea.

MARY-ELLEN. Taste this, Walter.

WALTER. I really don't want –

MARY-ELLEN. Taste it. It will be good for you.

WALTER. I don't want to –

MARY-ELLEN. Taste it!

(He drinks down the whole glass in one gulp just to spite her.)

MARY-ELLEN. Well?

WALTER. It's very good.

GARY. Actually it is.

MARY-ELLEN. Of course it is. Bao?

BAO. Good.

MARY-ELLEN. Thank you. Made it from scratch. It's a family recipe. And don't bother asking, I can't give it to you. You'd have to kill me first.

(silence)

Who needs more?

(She refills everyone's glasses.)

Why don't you put on some music, Gary?

GARY. Good idea.

MARY-ELLEN. Christmas music.

WALTER. No.

MARY-ELLEN. But, Walter, it's –

WALTER. I will break your hand if you put Christmas music on that stereo.

MARY-ELLEN. Fine.

GARY. I will look for something else.

(Everyone downs their eggnog.)

*(**MARY-ELLEN** refills their glasses.)*

MARY-ELLEN. Bao, I am so glad to meet you. How are you enjoying our country?

BAO. Well –

MARY-ELLEN. Are you finding it friendly?

BAO. I –

(**GARY** *searches the radio.*)

MARY-ELLEN. I like your hair. Who cuts it?

BAO. I do.

MARY-ELLEN. Really? I wish I could do that.

(**GARY** *lands on John Denver's "Sunshine On My Shoulders."*)*

MARY-ELLEN. That's good, Gary.

WALTER. No.

GARY. Why not?

WALTER. No.

(*More drinking by all.*)

(**GARY** *keeps searching the radio.*)

MARY-ELLEN. So tell me more about yourself, Bao? Are you doing OK?

BAO. What do you mean?

MARY-ELLEN. Life has sure thrown you for a loop, hasn't it? You have relatives here?

WALTER. Mary-Ellen –

MARY-ELLEN. What? It's Christmas –

(**GARY** *finally lands on "In the Summertime" by Mungo Jerry.*)*

MARY-ELLEN. Oh. Yes! I love this song. Turn it up, Gary.

(*He turns it up.*)

(**MARY-ELLEN** *begins to dance.*)

(**GARY** *joins him.*)

GARY. Walter loves to dance, don't you, Walter?

(*silence*)

---

*Please see Music Use Note on page 3.

(**WALTER** *drinks more egg nog.*)

GARY. C'mon. You know you want to.

WALTER. No I don't.

MARY-ELLEN. Do you dance, Bao?

BAO. Yes.

(**BAO** *hesitates.*)

MARY-ELLEN. Let's see it.

(*He finishes his egg nog, gets up and begins dancing.*)

(**WALTER** *sits on the couch. Watching. Grumpy.*)

(**GARY** *turns up the music.*)

(**WALTER**'s *legs move. Head moves.*)

(**MARY-ELLEN** *pulls* **WALTER** *off the couch, and he succumbs to the music.*)

(*They are all dancing.*)

(*Turns out,* **BAO** *is a very good dancer.*)

Wow Bao.

(*That makes her laugh.*)

Great!

(*They keep dancing. Trying to out dance each other's moves.*)

(*The more* **WALTER** *dances, the more frenetic he gets. Until he is crying and dancing at the same time.*)

(*He grabs the Christmas tree and pulls the plug from the wall, and throws it outside.*)

(*He keeps going until the house is trashed.*)

(**BAO**, **MARY-ELLEN** *and* **GARY** *gradually stops dancing, as they look what's happening around them.*)

(**WALTER** *grabs the large family portrait from the wall and begins to break it on the ground, but can't. He stops.*)

(**WALTER** *sets the portrait gently on the ground.*)

(**GARY** *stops the music.*)

(**WALTER** *exits.*)

(**MARY-ELLEN** *and* **GARY** *and* **BAO** *stare at each other.*)

GARY. Nothing like a little dancing to liven things up.

(**BAO** *tries to hang the portrait back where it was.*)

(**MARY-ELLEN** *looks out into the back yard.*)

MARY-ELLEN. That's it for the tree.

GARY. Why?

MARY-ELLEN. It's in the pool.

(*A car can be heard leaving offstage.*)

GARY. That's it for Walter.

(**GARY** *just looks at* **MARY-ELLEN.**)

MARY-ELLEN. What? I didn't know –

GARY. I told you this was a bad idea.

MARY-ELLEN. I just thought –

GARY. Why do you have to push things all the time, Mary-Ellen?

MARY-ELLEN. I don't push things –

GARY. Yes. You do.

MARY-ELLEN. Like what?

GARY. Everything.

(*silence*)

Everything.

(*silence*)

Why can't you just let things be, huh?

(*silence*)

MARY-ELLEN. I'll go find him.

GARY. I'm going.

MARY-ELLEN. I'll go –

GARY. He's *my* friend.

(*silence*)

MARY-ELLEN. OK then.

(MARY-ELLEN grabs her drink, and sits on the couch.)

(GARY looks at her, then exits.)

(BAO sits down with his drink. Looks at the mess around them.)

(They both drink. Not sure what to do next.)

(silence)

MARY-ELLEN. *(cont.)* Let me ask you something, Bao.

(silence)

Would you ask a woman like me to get married?

BAO. I, I don't understand.

(She moves closer to him.)

MARY-ELLEN. I don't want to get married. Really. I don't. I just want to be the type you could ask.

(silence)

MARY-ELLEN. You know what I mean?

BAO. No.

MARY-ELLEN. A woman just needs to know it's possible. That she's good enough. Beautiful enough. Young enough.

(silence)

You know?

(She kisses him.)

You know?

(She kisses him again.)

(She touches his face.)

MARY-ELLEN. You're very sweet.

BAO. Do that again. Please.

Scene Six

(A city park)

(Night)

(Christmas lights can be seen in the distance.)

(**WALTER** *sits on the ground.)*

(**GARY** *enters.)*

GARY. Here you are.

WALTER. Leave me alone.

GARY. I've been looking all over the place.

WALTER. Leave me alone, Gary.

(silence)

GARY. We shouldn't have forced ourselves on you. I'm sure, I'm sure this day is loaded with memories.

WALTER. You think?

GARY. I'm sorry.

WALTER. Isn't it bad enough the whole fucking neighbor-hood is covered in Christmas, everyone is celebrating with their families, and you have to come bring it in my house?

GARY. We were trying to – Mary-Ellen didn't – we didn't want you to sit alone –

WALTER. Why? What does it matter?

GARY. We didn't want you to feel sad.

WALTER. I'm sad!

GARY. I feel helpless –

WALTER. I'm sad! This is who I am. I'm sad and angry and alone. This is who I am.

GARY. No it's not.

WALTER. Yes it is! Look at me!

(silence)

GARY. It's not who you used to be.

WALTER. Lots of people aren't who they used to be. It happens all the time. The world is full of, of changed, sad people.

GARY. I guess.

WALTER. They peel themselves off the floor. And they survive.

(silence)

Without fucking Christmas trees. They get by.

GARY. OK.

(silence)

WALTER. And someday maybe, they even rise up again. Happy.

(silence)

GARY. I hope so.

(silence)

WALTER. You know, I have spent my entire life afraid that something horrible would happen to me. It would keep me up some nights, in a panic. Worrying about Margaret, the kids. The house. The business. But, I kept it a bay by just believing, I was different. I was special. "Nothing bad ever happens to Walter Wells…I've got it all under control. I'm safe. I'm special."

GARY. You are –

WALTER. I'm not.

GARY. You're the most joyous man I ever met. Nothing gets you down. You can make light of anything –

WALTER. I'm just like everyone else.

GARY. No. You're not.

WALTER. I am!…Stop trying to prevent me from changing. God. That's all you've done since the accident. Please. Just let me cave in like other people.

(silence)

Just let me be *this*. Let me be who I am now. OK?

GARY. It scares me.

WALTER. Why? You afraid you're going to catch it?

(silence)

GARY. Maybe.

(silence)

This whole thing has been out of my league.

(silence)

I'm sorry. I'm a terrible minister. I know that. I'm weak. I hate conflict. Everything scares. And I'm not cut out for much else really. Most things are out of my league, I think. The church doesn't seem to mind. They're good people. I make a good pot of coffee.

WALTER. Yes.

GARY. But I love you, Walter. And if I could give you back Margaret and the kids, I would. I'd wrestle God for them. I swear, I'd go up there and fight Him to my death, just to bring them back.

(silence)

I've been fighting Him every day since they died.

(silence)

Bastard. He took my best friends. My family.

(silence)

WALTER. Well. I appreciate that.

(silence)

(WALTER *is unsure what to say or do next.)*

(Finally.)

I guess this is my life now, huh?

GARY. I'm sorry.

(silence)

WALTER. I don't belong here anymore.

(silence)

I want to be happy.

Scene Seven

(Wells living room)

MARY-ELLEN. Well.

*(**MARY-ELLEN** and **BAO** dress.)*

That lit the old yule log, didn't it?

BAO. What?

MARY-ELLEN. Christmas fire.

(silence)

BAO. I don't understand…

MARY-ELLEN. That was fun.

BAO. Oh. Yes. Fun.

(silence)

MARY-ELLEN. Who knows what you think of me now.

BAO. I think you are very nice.

(She buttons her blouse.)

MARY-ELLEN. I don't know what gets into me sometimes.

BAO. What?

MARY-ELLEN. Nothing like a little shame to sober a girl up.

(silence)

Never too old for that

BAO. You are beautiful.

MARY-ELLEN. Thank you.

BAO. And tall.

MARY-ELLEN. Thank you. Really. But please. You don't need to start that.

BAO. Start what?

MARY-ELLEN. I appreciate the compliment. Really. But you know this can't happen again.

BAO. Oh. OK. Yes. Of course.

MARY-ELLEN. Sweet as you are, I'd probably swallow you up anyway.

(silence)

MARY-ELLEN. I lost an earring somewhere around here…

BAO. You are the first woman. Since my wife.

(She finds it on the floor.)

MARY-ELLEN. Found it.

BAO. I have only sex with my wife.

MARY-ELLEN. Really?

BAO. Yes.

MARY-ELLEN. Handsome guy like you?

BAO. Yes.

MARY-ELLEN. How'd I do?

BAO. Good. Very good.

MARY-ELLEN. Well. Thank you. I aim to please.

(She pushes back her hair, and a laugh.)

BAO. What about me?

MARY-ELLEN. What –

BAO. Am I OK?

MARY-ELLEN. Oh. Gosh. Yes. Wonderful.

(silence)

Very tender.

(silence)

Your wife was a lucky woman.

(silence)

BAO. I hope so.

MARY-ELLEN. I'm sorry, Bao.

(silence)

Stupid war.

(silence)

I don't know who to blame anymore. Do you?

(long silence)

Well.

*(**MARY-ELLEN** smiles. Changing the subject.)*

MARY-ELLEN. *(cont.)* Is there anything more awkward than drunken sex with a complete stranger?

BAO. I don't know.

(She puts on her shoes.)

MARY-ELLEN. Well, actually…sometimes it can feel like you've known that person your whole life. You know what I mean?

BAO. I think so.

MARY-ELLEN. I guess that's makes it awkward too.

BAO. Yes.

(She straightens her skirt.)

MARY-ELLEN. That kind of thing scares the shit out of me. Really. It's too heavy. I just can't live that way. All emotional all the time. It's too much.

(She fixes her hair.)

*(**BAO** looks at the small photo of his family.)*

I'm better with the men who just want to have fun.

(They are fully dressed, on opposite sides of the stage.)

BAO. *(in Vietnamese)* Sing loi em. Anh hoi-hun da-baw em.
("I'm sorry, my love. I should have never left you.")

Scene Eight

(February, 1976)

(Wells Appliance)

(WALTER *gather the very last of his papers.)*

(The phone rings.)

WALTER. Wells Appliance…Oh, hello Carl, no, I'm sorry. I guess you didn't hear…I've sold the business….Yeah… well, things change….Milton Appliance might have that, or Sears…Uh huh…Of course, sure, no problem…thank you…yes, thank you, you too, Carl…Take care…bye bye.

(The phone rings.)

Wells Appliance. You do realize this isn't a grocery store, kid? Uh huh…But, you're in luck, I do have Prince Albert in a can…Well, who is *this*?…Tim Who?…Well, I have to know your last name before I tell the Prince who is looking for him, don't I?…Tiny Tim, so is Tiny your last name or first?…Well, I have to be specific, don't I? Prince Albert is a touchy guy, and things aren't going so well in the kingdom. War, famine, plague…Plague's a disease. Comes from rats… How old are you Tiny Tim?…It does too matter. Albert is a stickler for details. He likes to know Exactly who is looking for him and how old they are…You want me to get him or not?…Well, don't get short with me, you're the one who called…Thirteen?…Shouldn't you be in school?…What is it, a cough, a flu, what?…Uh huh…I see, and your mother let you stay home for that?… Where's she work?…Oh, The Jolly Knight? I like that restaurant. So does Prince Albert, he and the Knight go way back…Uh huh…really?…Sounds like you're a bit of trouble maker, Tiny Tim?…Where's your Dad?… Oh. He did…I see…Oh…Well, I'm sure he'll come back, right?…Oh, don't cry Tiny Tim….It's not? What is it then?…David…Don't cry…David, don't cry… I'm sorry I brought up your dad…Let me get Prince

Albert...Here he comes. He's coming to the phone...
He is too. He's grabbing the phone.

(British accent)

WALTER. *(cont.)* Prince Albert here. Is this Sir David?...Is it
true you've been asking for me?...Is there something
I can do for you then?...You want someone to let me
out?...Well, I've been let out. Didn't get the message?...
Good news travels slow, I guess. I've been out of that
can for some time now, though I'm not sure how I like
it out here in the cold...My father left the family, you
see...yes, and he left me the kingdom which I don't
really want. It frightens me. The crown. The respon-
sibility. All the people. But, I guess I have to accept it.
That's what we do, you know, we men. We accept our
lot in life. The good with the bad. We pull ourselves
together and we act brave and carry on. Head held
high. Because even if we don't feel brave, someday it
will catch up with us. The bravery will find us. And the
courage. It will find us, if we just keep acting like it's
ours. Right? It will be ours someday, David...Right?...
Are you still there...David?...Yes, well, I'll let you go
then. Eat some soup or something, alright?...You don't
like soup? Eat a sandwich then...Crackers, crackers are
fine...And remember to be brave. That can take you a
long way, young man...You're not?...How old are you
then? You're full of surprises – Eleven...Well, eleven is
the perfect age for crackers and courage...it is. Many
great people have lived on that, and nothing else, and
triumphed...I swear...OK...I will be thinking about
you. OK then. Be well, Sir David.

(He hangs up.)

(He unplugs the phone.)

*(He grabs the phone, and the rest of his papers, and
exits.)*

Scene Nine

(Wells living room)

(March, 1976)

(Vietnamese music plays.)

(Half the room is packed in boxes. The large family portrait leans against a chair.)

(WALTER *enters with empty boxes.)*

(He packs up the photo albums. Opens one, and quickly closes it.)

(Every object he touches, he must quickly pack.)

(The doorbell rings.)

WALTER. Come in!

(It rings again.)

Come in! It's open.

(BAO *enters.)*

WALTER. Oh. Hi, Bao. Did you lose your key?

BAO. I know you like people to ring the bell. When you're home.

WALTER. Thanks.

BAO. You like this music?

WALTER. I do.

BAO. You can have it.

WALTER. No…

BAO. Please. Keep it. I want you to have it.

WALTER. No.

BAO. Please. I insist.

(BAO *sets the key on a box.)*

I will leave the key. For the next family.

WALTER. They seem real nice. Two kids. He's a plumber, I think. Which is a good thing, because the plumbing has never been very good in this house. He can fix that.

BAO. Easy for him.

WALTER. Plumbing's a good skill. You'll always have a job.

(silence)

BAO. What is your job going to be? You'll need money.

WALTER. I'm going to see how long I can live off the house and business money.

BAO. How long is that?

WALTER. I guess I'll find out.

BAO. Where are you going?

WALTER. Don't know yet.

BAO. You have no plan. You need a plan.

WALTER. I'm just going to get in the car and drive.

BAO. Where? Do you have a map. You need a map –

WALTER. Maybe I'll make my way to New York. I've only been there once.

BAO. New York City?

WALTER. Yeah.

BAO. Isn't it dangerous? And cold in the winter? You don't want to go there.

WALTER. It's not dangerous. And I was born in Wisconsin. I don't mind the cold. Though I never thought I'd leave California. You have come to the right place. You got lucky coming here. This is the most beautiful state in this country. Don't let anyone tell you different.

BAO. OK.

WALTER. This is the good life right here.

(He tapes up a box.)

You'll be working as a doctor here in no time. Southern California has got everything you need to succeed. Everything.

(**BAO** watches **WALTER** finish up taping the box.)

BAO. It won't have my friend.

WALTER. Am I your friend?

BAO. Please forgive me.

(silence)

BAO. Forgive me.

(**WALTER** *puts out his hand.*)

WALTER. Friend.

BAO. Forgive me.

(**WALTER** *keeps out his hand.*)

WALTER. We're looking at the future now, aren't we?

BAO. Walter –

WALTER. The future.

(**BAO** *hugs him, surprising both of them.*)

WALTER. It's going to be so great we won't recognize ourselves. Right?

BAO. Right.

WALTER. It will be wonderful.

BAO. Wonderful.

WALTER. We'll be so happy.

BAO. Happy.

WALTER. We're going to look back someday and see strangers standing here.

BAO. Strangers.

WALTER. "Who were those old sad sacks?"

BAO. Bao and Walter.

WALTER. "Who had those long faces?"

BAO. Bao and Walter.

WALTER. "Crybabies."

(**WALTER** *turns to continue to packing.*)

BAO. Please don't go.

Scene Ten

(April, 1976)

(Outside the church)

(GARY and MARY-ELLEN enter kissing. Both are a little tipsy.)

(GARY finally pulls away and combs his hair.)

(MARY-ELLEN cleans the lipstick from his face, then reapplies fresh lipstick to herself.)

MARY-ELLEN. You look handsome.

GARY. I do?

MARY-ELLEN. Almost as handsome as they day we met. I couldn't take my eyes of you.

GARY. You were getting married.

MARY-ELLEN. It was very distracting.

GARY. You're not going to leave me, are you?

MARY-ELLEN. What?

GARY. Well, what if Tim Conway walks by –

(WALTER enters, out of breath, with a bouquet of flowers. A camera around his neck.)

WALTER. Sorry I'm late. It took longer than I thought.

GARY. Did you get it?

(He hold up the keys.)

WALTER. I am now the proud owner of a Datsun.

(They look in the distance.)

MARY-ELLEN. Is that it?

WALTER. Yep.

GARY. Where?

WALTER. They didn't give me much of a trade in for the Chrysler.

GARY. It's not very big, is it.

WALTER. Great gas mileage.

GARY. Sure, sure.

WALTER. It's got a lot of zip.

MARY-ELLEN. Does it have that new car smell?

WALTER. Yep.

MARY-ELLEN. I love that.

GARY. It's very compact.

> *(The men keep looking at the car.)*

> Bet it's easy to park.

WALTER. Oh yeah. I can fit anywhere.

MARY-ELLEN. I drove by your house this morning, Walter. Looks like the new people moved in last night. They put some god-awful yard animals in the front yard. Fake deer or pheasant or something.

WALTER. It's their house now.

MARY-ELLEN. It will always be your house in my mind. I don't know why you had to sell it to people with tacky tastes. That just adds insult to injury.

> *(**GARY** checks his watch.)*

GARY. We still want to do this thing?

MARY-ELLEN. Aren't you proud of Gary, Walter? All grown up.

GARY. Gonna give it the old college try.

WALTER. I, uh, I'm sorry. I don't think I'm going to be able to make it.

MARY-ELLEN. What?

GARY. Walter –

WALTER. I just came by to say congratulations.

GARY. No…C'mon.

> *(He gives her the flowers.)*

WALTER. I'm going to hit the road today.

GARY & MARY-ELLEN. *Today?*

MARY-ELLEN. I am the first woman to get this man to the altar, and you aren't even going to be here to see it?

GARY. You can't.

WALTER. I'm sorry –

GARY. Walter –

WALTER. You don't need me.

GARY. I do. I need you. I'm very confused. I need some water.

WALTER. You can do it.

GARY. I hired a Minister in there that scares the shit out of me. He's very religious.

MARY-ELLEN. He needs you, Walter.

WALTER. You don't need me in there crying my eyes out. Making a scene.

GARY. I do –

WALTER. I want to head out before it gets too late. I'm going to drive one last drive along the coast. Say goodbye to the Pacific.

MARY-ELLEN. Do you have to? Now?

WALTER. Yeah.

GARY. My head hurts.

MARY-ELLEN. I told you four Bloody Marys would hurt.

GARY. You had four.

MARY-ELLEN. I'm the bride. I need the vegetables.

(She checks her pocket.)

MARY-ELLEN. Oh dear.

(She checks her purse.)

MARY-ELLEN. I think I might have left your ring at the bar.

GARY. I told you the bartender didn't want to try it on.

WALTER. Let me get your picture.

GARY. I think I need to lie down.

*(**WALTER** backs away and gets the camera ready.)*

WALTER. Look at you two, you're the perfect couple. Like starry-eyed teenagers. Smile now.

*(**MARY-ELLEN** and **GARY** push smiles.)*

Beautiful.

(He takes the picture.)

WALTER. *(cont.)* One more for good luck. Smile like you really mean it this time. It's your wedding day, for Christ's sake.

(**MARY-ELLEN** *and* **GARY** *smiles almost break the camera they are so big.)*

Perfect.

(**WALTER** *takes the picture.)*

I'll send that to you. You're going to want to get it framed.

(**BAO** *enters with a small suitcase, and a map.)*

WALTER. You ready?

BAO. Yes.

WALTER. OK then.

BAO. Hello Mary-Ellen.

MARY-ELLEN. You're going with, Walter?

BAO. I am.

GARY. How come he gets to go?

WALTER. I'm showing him the rest of the country.

BAO. I got the map.

GARY. I've never seen the country.

WALTER. Mary-Ellen is going to show you plenty.

MARY-ELLEN. That's right.

GARY. *(quietly to* **WALTER***)* You're not letting him ive-dray *(pig-latin for drive)*, are you?

WALTER. Wait. I have one more thing. Hold on. I'll be right back.

(**WALTER** *runs offstage.)*

GARY. I like to travel.

(**BAO** *and* **MARY-ELLEN** *smile awkwardly at each other.)*

MARY-ELLEN. I wish you the best, Bao. Really.

BAO. Yes. You too.

GARY. I'm his best friend.

MARY-ELLEN. I hope everything works out for you.

BAO. Thank you. Congratulations on your marriage.

MARY-ELLEN. Thank you.

GARY. I could have gone.

MARY-ELLEN. Some things just come unexpected. What the hell, right?

BAO. Right.

GARY. There's lots of places I've never seen.

MARY-ELLEN. I like your shirt. Nice pattern.

BAO. It's new.

MARY-ELLEN. And it won't wrinkle. That material is good for travel.

GARY. I like to travel.

*(**GARY** wipes his forehead with his handkerchief.)*

I'm thirsty. I need to lie down.

*(**WALTER** hurries in, carrying the large family portrait from his living room.)*

WALTER. OK. Here we are.

*(He gives it to **GARY**.)*

I want you to have it.

GARY. I couldn't –

WALTER. Please. I can't take it with me. And I can't seem to put it in storage. So, I just…

MARY-ELLEN. We'll hold on to it for you.

GARY. Of course.

*(**GARY** takes it.)*

WALTER. I, I want you to have it.

MARY-ELLEN. We'll take good care of it.

GARY. I'm honored, Walter.

WALTER. Thanks. Wonderful. OK then.

(He claps his hands.)

(**WALTER** *gives* **GARY** *and* **MARY-ELLEN** *a quick hug.*)

WALTER. *(cont.)* Take care of yourselves. You can do this, Gary.

GARY. I can?

WALTER. It's not out of your league.

GARY. It's not?

(*He picks up Bao's bag.*)

WALTER. Onward.

(**BAO** *shakes* **GARY** *and* **MARY-ELLEN**'s *hands.*)

BAO. Good-bye.

MARY-ELLEN. Bye.

WALTER. I'll send you that picture. Congratulations again. It's all going to work out great. I just know it.

(**WALTER** *and* **BAO** *quickly wave and exit.*)

(**MARY-ELLEN** *and* **GARY** *stand rather stunned.*)

(*The family portrait hangs awkwardly in one of* **GARY**'s *hands. He and* **MARY-ELLEN** *are trying to smile; the California sun is bright in their eyes as they are waving good-bye.*)

(*The sound of a car starting, then driving away off-stage.*)

(**MARY-ELLEN** *and* **GARY** *are still waving good-bye as lights fade.*)

End of Play

OTHER TITLES AVAILABLE FROM SAMUEL FRENCH

CAPTIVE
Jan Buttram

Comedy / 2m, 1f / Interior

A hilarious take on a father/daughter relationship, this off beat comedy combines foreign intrigue with down home philosophy. Sally Pound flees a bad marriage in New York and arrives at her parent's home in Texas hoping to borrow money from her brother to pay a debt to gangsters incurred by her husband. Her elderly parents are supposed to be vacationing in Israel, but she is greeted with a shotgun aimed by her irascible father who has been left home because of a minor car accident and is not at all happy to see her. When a news report indicates that Sally's mother may have been taken captive in the Middle East, Sally's hard-nosed brother insists that she keep father home until they receive definite word, and only then will he loan Sally the money. Sally fails to keep father in the dark, and he plans a rescue while she finds she is increasingly unable to skirt the painful truths of her life. The ornery father and his loveable but slightly-dysfunctional daughter come to a meeting of hearts and minds and solve both their problems.

OTHER TITLES AVAILABLE FROM SAMUEL FRENCH

TAKE HER, SHE'S MINE

Phoebe and Henry Ephron

Comedy / 11m, 6f / Various Sets

Art Carney and Phyllis Thaxter played the Broadway roles of parents of two typical American girls enroute to college. The story is based on the wild and wooly experiences the authors had with their daughters, Nora Ephron and Delia Ephron, themselves now well known writers. The phases of a girl's life are cause for enjoyment except to fearful fathers. Through the first two years, the authors tell us, college girls are frightfully sophisticated about all departments of human life. Then they pass into the "liberal" period of causes and humanitarianism, and some into the intellectual lethargy of beatniksville. Finally, they start to think seriously of their lives as grown ups. It's an experience in growing up, as much for the parents as for the girls.

"A warming comedy. A delightful play about parents vs kids. It's loaded with laughs. It's going to be a smash hit."
– *New York Mirror*

OTHER TITLES AVAILABLE FROM SAMUEL FRENCH

MURDER AMONG FRIENDS
Bob Barry

Comedy Thriller / 4m, 2f / Interior

Take an aging, exceedingly vain actor; his very rich wife; a double dealing, double loving agent, plunk them down in an elegant New York duplex and add dialogue crackling with wit and laughs, and you have the basic elements for an evening of pure, sophisticated entertainment. Angela, the wife and Ted, the agent, are lovers and plan to murder Palmer, the actor, during a contrived robbery on New Year's Eve. But actor and agent are also lovers and have an identical plan to do in the wife. A murder occurs, but not one of the planned ones.

"Clever, amusing, and very surprising."
— *New York Times*

"A slick, sophisticated show that is modern and very funny."
— WABC TV

SAMUELFRENCH.COM

OTHER TITLES AVAILABLE FROM SAMUEL FRENCH

THE RIVERS AND RAVINES
Heather McDonald

Drama / 9m, 5f / Unit Set

Originally produced to acclaim by Washington D.C.'s famed Arena Stage. This is an engrossing political drama about the contemporary farm crisis in America and its effect on rural communities.

"A haunting and emotionally draining play. A community of farmers and ranchers in a small Colorado town disintegrates under the weight of failure and thwarted ambitions. Most of the farmers, their spouses, children, clergyman, banker and greasy spoon proprietress survive, but it is survival without triumph. This is an *Our Town* for the 80's."
– *The Washington Post*

OTHER TITLES AVAILABLE FROM SAMUEL FRENCH

JITNEY
August Wilson

Drama / 8m, 1f / Interiors
Set in 1970 in the Hill District of Pittsburgh that is served by a makeshift taxi company, Jitney is a beautiful addition to the author's decade by decade cycle of plays about the black American experience in the twentieth century.

"Could be described as just a lot of men sitting around talking. But the talk has such varied range and musicality, and it is rendered with such stylish detail, that a complete urban symphony emerges.... Drivers return from jobs with stories that summon an entire ethos.... Thoroughly engrossing, *Jitney* holds us in charmed captivity."
– *New York Times*

"Explosive... Crackles with theatrical energy."
– *New York Daily News*

Award Winning!
New York Drama Critics Award for Best New Play
Outer Critics Circle Award for Outstanding Off Broadway Play

SAMUELFRENCH.COM

OTHER TITLES AVAILABLE FROM SAMUEL FRENCH

OUTRAGE
Itamar Moses

Drama / 8m, 2f / Unit Set

In Ancient Greece, Socrates is accused of corrupting the young with his practice of questioning commonly held beliefs. In Renaissance Italy, a simple miller named Menocchio runs afoul of the Inquisition when he develops his own theory of the cosmos. In Nazi Germany, the playwright Bertolt Brecht is persecuted for work that challenges authority. And in present day New England, a graduate student finds himself in the center of a power struggle over the future of the University. An irreverent epic that spans thousands of years, *Outrage* explores the power of martyrdom, the power of theatre, and how the revolutionary of one era become the tyrant of the next.

SAMUELFRENCH.COM